INSPiRE

I0896506

IAIN ARMITAGE

BY JOANNE MATTERN

AMICUS LEARNING

Inspire is published by
Amicus Learning, an imprint of Amicus
P.O. Box 227
Mankato, MN 56002
www.amicuspublishing.us

Copyright © 2026 Amicus.
International copyright reserved in all countries.
No part of this book may be reproduced in any form
without written permission from the publisher.

Editor: Ana Brauer
Series Designer: Kathleen Petelinsek
Book Designer and Photo Researcher: Emily Dietz

Library of Congress Cataloging-in-Publication Data
Names: Mattern, Joanne, 1963- author
Title: Iain Armitage / by Joanne Mattern.
Description: Mankato, MN : Amicus Learning, an imprint of Amicus, 2026. | Series: Inspire | Includes bibliographical references and index. | Audience: Ages 5–9 | Audience: Grades 2–3 | Summary: "From theater fan to TV star! Discover how child actor Iain Armitage went from making YouTube videos to starring in *Young Sheldon*. This engaging biography includes a table of contents, glossary, further resources, and index"—Provided by publisher.
Identifiers: LCCN 2025011930 (print) | LCCN 2025011931 (ebook) | ISBN 9798892008594 library binding | ISBN 9798892009256 paperback | ISBN 9798892009911 ebook
Subjects: LCSH: Armitage, Iain—Juvenile literature | Television actors and actresses—United States—Biography—Juvenile literature | LCGFT: Biographies
Classification: LCC PN2287.A686 M38 2026 (print) | LCC PN2287.A686 (ebook) | DDC 791.4302/8092 [B]—dc23/eng/20250408
LC record available at https://lccn.loc.gov/2025011930
LC ebook record available at https://lccn.loc.gov/2025011931

Photo Credits: Alamy Stock Photo/Album, 12, Entertainment Pictures, 17, WENN, 6, ZUMA Press, 5; Associated Press/Juan Rico, cover; Getty Images/CBS Photo Archive, 15, Jon Kopaloff, 16, Kevin Mazur, 9, Larry Busacca, 10, NDZ/Star Max, 19, Tasos Katopodis, 20; Shutterstock/ Travis Potter, 18

Every effort has been made to contact copyright holders for material reproduced in this book. Any omissions will be rectified in subsequent printings if notice is given to the publisher.

Printed in the United States of America

Table of Contents

A Young Star

Iain Armitage is a young American actor. For seven years, he played Sheldon Cooper on the TV show *Young Sheldon*. Fans loved Armitage's energy. He did a great job playing a child who is a **genius**.

Iain Armitage is best known for his role in *Young Sheldon* (2017–24).

Armitage learned about acting early thanks to his dad, a theater producer.

Born to Perform

Armitage was born on July 5, 2008. He was born in Savannah, Georgia. Both of his parents worked in theater and movies. It was natural for Armitage to be an actor, as well.

FAMILY TIES

Armitage is an only child. But he has many cousins.

Welcome to YouTube

Armitage went to his first play when he was just three years old. He loved it! A few years later, he started his own YouTube channel. It was called “Iain Loves Theatre.” He **reviewed** plays.

Armitage was often invited backstage at Broadway shows he reviewed.

Because of his YouTube channel, Armitage got to attend the 2016 Tony Awards.

Discovered

When Armitage was about six years old, **agents** saw his channel. They thought he would be a great actor on TV. Armitage had a big **personality**. He also loved to talk. After talking it over with his parents, he said yes.

Armitage played Ziggy, a main character's son, in *Big Little Lies*.

Armitage on Screen

It did not take long for Armitage to be on TV. In 2017, the nine-year-old was **cast** in a TV show called *Big Little Lies*. Later that year, he was in a movie called *The Glass Castle*. Then Armitage got big news.

FIRST BREAK

Armitage's first TV appearance was on an episode of *Law & Order: Special Victims Unit* in 2017.

Young Sheldon

In 2017, Armitage won the lead role of Sheldon Cooper in the TV show *Young Sheldon*. Fans already knew Sheldon Cooper. The character was in a hit show called *The Big Bang Theory*. Armitage played Sheldon as a boy.

BLOND OR BROWN?
Armitage dyed his blond hair brown to play Sheldon Cooper.

Armitage played Sheldon Cooper for seven seasons of *Young Sheldon*.

Armitage attended the 2024 Kids' Choice Awards with costars Raegan Revord (middle) and Montana Jordan (right).

A Hit Show

Young Sheldon was a big hit! Fans loved the story of this very smart character and his loving family. Armitage had fun. He and other kids on the show became good friends. They loved going to amusement parks together.

STARRING HIS VOICE

Armitage has also done voice work in the movies *Scoob!* (2020) and *Paw Patrol: The Movie* (2021).

Inspiring Others

Armitage is known for being kind. He tries to make the world a better place. He is part of the actor's union, SAG-AFTRA. In 2023, he joined a strike with other actors. They wanted fair pay for shows and movies on streaming services.

DID YOU KNOW?
Armitage got his pilot's license after *Young Sheldon* ended in 2024.

In 2023, Armitage marched with other actors during the SAG-AFTRA strike.

In 2025, Armitage went to a special event to support the arts.

Looking to the Future

Armitage has big plans for the future. He would love to be in an action film. One thing is for sure. We will be seeing more of this young actor in the years to come!

SUPER STATS

IAIN ARMITAGE

Birthday: July 15, 2008

Birthplace: Savannah, GA

TV Roles: *Young Sheldon* (2017–2024), *Big Little Lies* (2017–2019), *Law & Order: Special Victims Unit* (2017)

Film Roles: *The Glass Castle* (2017), *Our Souls at Night* (2017), *Paw Patrol: The Movie* (voice, 2021), *Scoob!* (voice, 2020)

AWARDS

Kids' Choice Awards: 2024

Family Film Awards: 2024

GLOSSARY

agent A person who gets jobs for actors and other performers.

cast To get a part in a show, movie, or play.

genius An unusual ability to think or create in ways that go far beyond what most people can do.

personality The set of qualities that makes a person different from others.

review To describe your feelings about something.

READ MORE

Cohen, Ivan. **The Big Bang Theory: A Matter of Friendship.** Little, Brown and Company, 2024.

Waxman, Laura Hamilton. **Cool Kid Actors.** Minneapolis: Lerner Publications, 2020.

ON THE WEB

IMDb: Iain Armitage
https://www.imdb.com/name/nm8071137/?ref_=nmawd_ov

Official YouTube Channel
https://www.youtube.com/c/iainlovestheatre

Every effort has been made to ensure that these websites are appropriate for children. However, because of the nature of the Internet, it is impossible to guarantee that these sites will remain active indefinitely or that their contents will not be altered.

INDEX

About the Author

Joanne Mattern is the author of hundreds of nonfiction books for children. Her favorite subjects are biographies, sports, animals, and history. Joanne loves learning new things and sharing that knowledge with young readers! She lives in New York State with her family.